Amazon Kindle Fire HD 10 User Guide

The Complete Manual Book on How to Master Your Kindle HD 10 Tablet

Carlos Allen

Copyright 2017 by Carlos Allen - All rights reserved

The following book is reproduced with the goal of providing information that is as accurate and reliable as possible. Regardless, purchasing this book can be seen as consent to the fact that both the publisher and the author of this book are in no way experts on the topics discussed within and that any recommendations or suggestions that are made herein are for entertainment purposes only. Professionals should be consulted as needed prior to undertaking any of the action endorsed herein.

This declaration is deemed fair and valid by both the American Bar Association and the Committee of Publishers Association and is legally binding throughout the United States.

Furthermore, the transmission, duplication or reproduction of any of the following work including specific information will be considered an illegal act irrespective of if it is done electronically or in print. This extends to creating a secondary or tertiary copy of the work or a recorded copy and is only allowed with express written consent from the Publisher. All additional rights reserved.

The information in the following pages is broadly considered to be a truthful and accurate account of facts and as such any inattention, use or misuse of the information in question by the reader will render any resulting actions solely under their purview. There are no scenarios in which the publisher or the original author of this work can be in any fashion deemed liable for any hardship or damages that may befall them after undertaking information described herein.

Additionally, the information in the following pages is intended only for informational purposes and should thus be thought of as universal. As befitting its nature, it is presented without assurance regarding its prolonged validity or interim quality. Trademarks that are mentioned are done without written consent and can in no way be considered an endorsement from the trademark holder.

TABLE OF CONTENTS

INTRODUCTION 1

CHAPTER 1: WHAT IT'S LIKE 5

Display 6

Sound 13

Storage 15

RAM and Processor 17

Apps 19

Camera 25

Battery 28

Appearance 32

Budget 34

CHAPTER 2: SETTING UP YOUR TABLET 35

Choosing Settings 36

Registering Your Device 37

Alexa 37

Adding Email and Other Accounts 38

Creating Calendar Events 39

Downloading Apps 40

Hooking up to WiFi 41

Getting Games and Other Content 42

CHAPTER 3: DISPLAY ISSUES 45

Screen Stays Black 46

Screen Flickers 47

Screen Haze 48

CHAPTER 4: BATTERY ISSUES 51

Refusing to Charge 51

Overheating 56

Getting It Wet 60

CHAPTER 5: SOFTWARE AND CONNECTIVITY ISSUES 65

App Crashing 66

Freezing During Use 67

Failure to Start Up.. 70

Not Connecting to PC....................................... 71

Not Connecting to WiFi.................................... 75

CHAPTER 6: SOUND ISSUES 81

No Sound.. 81

CHAPTER 7: HARDWARE ISSUES 85

MicroSD Card Not Working 86

Shutting Down on Its Own 87

Keyboard Typing Erratically 89

CHAPTER 8: CARING FOR YOUR DEVICE........91

Invest in a Case 92

Invest in Screen Protection............................. 94

How to Clean 96

Watch Your Downloads 98

Use Security 101

How to Charge Your Device Properly 103

CONCLUSION **107**

Introduction

Hello there! Have you seen the new Kindle Fire 10 and you want it now? Or did you actually make the leap and purchase one? I bet you're excited to get to know your new device and make it work for you. But you probably also have tons of questions. This book is your guide to the Kindle Fire 10 and everything you need to know about it. By the end of this book, you will be able to determine if you should buy this, or how to use it and what to do if things go wrong if you already own one.

First, we will delve into this device in its full splendor. We will go beyond the simple

Amazon Kindle Fire HD 10 User Guide

product specifications you can find with a simple Google search, and we will actually explore this device. As someone who owns a Kindle Fire 10, I can walk you through this device's capabilities and apps. I will explain what makes this device worth the purchase…or why you maybe should not buy it. For example, if you are a big gamer, this may not be the device for you. If you do tons of photo editing or graphic design work, the software on this device may not be able to keep up. But if you are a general Kindle user looking for a tablet to surf the web, watch videos, save data, send emails, and such on, you can count on this device.

Then, we will go more into detail about what to expect from your device. We will cover how to set it up. The first time you unwrap your Kindle and start to set it up is an exciting time. You want to make your device match your needs. So you want to avoid the frustration of not knowing how to navigate this device and how to set it up. This is your guide to how to set up without diminishing the excitement and joy of owning a new device.

Now all is well, but what if something goes wrong? You know how electronic devices are. Sometimes things go wrong and you can't figure out how to fix it. We will go into troubleshooting. You will learn how to treat sound and display issues, software glitches, battery issues, and the like. If anything does go wrong, you will not panic or give up. You will just be able to fix this device with little headache.

Amazon Kindle Fire HD 10 User Guide

This guide covers everything you will want to know. From one user to another, this guide is written to make using your new Kindle Fire 10 a breeze. It may also help you form a solid purchase decision if you are still on the fence about buying this device.

Chapter 1: What It's Like

Before you invest in the Kindle Fire 10, you obviously want to know what this device is like. What is like to own? What does it feel like to use? What does it look like? Here, you will learn all about what it's like to own a Kindle Fire 10.

We won't go into product specifications here, because you can find that with a simple search on Amazon. We want to talk about the more interesting things – the things you wouldn't know unless you owned this tablet yourself. Beyond product specifications, we are going to delve into the actual facts. What is it really like having a Kindle Fire 10?

Display

The display is obviously one of the most important parts of the tablet experience. Without a good display, you can't enjoy videos, games, or even video chats. A good display is crucial to having a great tablet experience that meets all of your tablet needs and expectations. The Kindle Fire 10 has an upgraded display that is geared to meet even better visual expectations than previous versions of the Kindle Fire device.

The Kindle Fire 10 boasts a great 10.1-inch display with 1920 x 1200 pixels of resolution. Now this specification may mean nothing to you, so let's delve into how important pixels of resolution can be. You can determine if this display is sufficient for your needs based on this information.

Most tablets have either seven-inch or ten-inch screens. There are some with massive twenty-inch screens, and some with tiny five-inch screens, but seven or ten inches are the most common on the market. Like the Kindle Fire 10, you will find that a ten-inch screen makes the device altogether larger and bulkier. The larger the screen, the larger the device, however, having a ten-inch screen can offer some advantages over smaller and sleeker seven-inch devices. A larger screen offers far more room to see the images you have on your device. It is nicer for viewing from angles, and it offers some more comfort in playing games. The Kindle Fire 10's ten-inch screen is therefore better for image and video viewing, gaming, and other needs than that of smaller tablets.

Aspect ratio is another crucial part of viewing images. Without the right aspect ratio, images don't appear correctly and can become strangely distorted. All the aspect ratio is the ratio between its horizontal width and its vertical height. The Kindle Fire 10 has a rather common aspect ratio of 16:*10* aspect ratio. This means that it is sixteen inches by ten inches. This aspect ratio is set up to ensure that images appear correctly without the odd distortion. In some images that require a vastly different aspect ratio, images may not appear at their best. But since 16 x 10 is common, you will find that it is quite adequate for almost all images that you will encounter in your average tablet use. Only certain games and graphic design work may require a different aspect ratio.

Now what about that pixels of resolution? The 1920 x 1200 pixels of resolution basically means that there are 224 pixels per inch of the device. So for every inch you are looking at, you are seeing 224 pixels. Having more pixel density equals better image clarity, so this tablet offers pretty great picture clarity. In fact, a pixel density of greater than 200 (which fits the Kindle Fire 10) is as detailed as a printed book.

A higher resolution is a good thing as it means that you can see more detail. In the average tablet, you might just need enough resolution to read some emails and display some WebPages. For that kind of requirement, you only require up to 480 x 480 pixels. So you can do a lot more with this higher resolution. You can view WebPages, HTML emails, and even videos and games with this higher resolution. The Kindle Fire 10's resolution is more than adequate for the average person's graphic needs.

In fact, the Kindle Fire 10 is ideal for various things like reading emails, reading eBooks, and viewing WebPages in full detail. Forget having to struggle to view grainy pictures, or having pictures cut off altogether, as you browse the web. The issues you may face viewing WebPages on a mobile phone because of its low resolution are solved with this tablet. You will find that viewing what you need to look at is a breeze.

Chapter 1: What It's Like

Its flat face does not diminish its ability for viewing under various different angles. When you view things on this tablet, you will find that you can visit many angles. Laying down and watching a Youtube video on this tablet? You can with this large and well-angled screen. Trying to view it from the side as you jog or scrub the floors of your house? Well, you can. The versatility offered by this is astounding and very convenient.

Fortunately, you can adjust your viewing angles. You can view things in portrait mode, or in landscape mode. Portrait is straight up and down, or vertical; landscape is long ways, or horizontal. This can make this tablet more customizable to your viewing needs. However, changing these viewing modes can be a bit cumbersome, especially when you are active and using the tablet at the same time. This is why the Kindle Fire 10's wide viewing angles are quite helpful. You can see a lot on this tablet in either portrait or landscape, without having to adjust viewing modes.

Nevertheless, there are tablets with better displays, such as the iPad. This is probably not the best tablet for someone with intensely high graphic needs, such as a hardcore gamer or a graphic designer hoping to work on a tablet. But for this price, you get a display that enables you to watch videos, play simple games, read eBooks, and view WebPages. This tablet is more than capable of meeting basic viewing needs, provided that you don't rely heavily on excellent graphics. If you don't want to pay an arm and a leg, and you don't have to use your tablet for extremely detailed graphics, then the Kindle Fire 10 is more than enough for you.

Sound

Now the sound is also important. If you are listening to music, watching videos, playing games, or running video chats and Skype calls, you obviously want to be able to hear. Some tablets are not well-suited for listening to sound, but the Kindle Fire 10 boasts a pair of Dolby Atmus-tuned speakers.

So what does this mean? It means that Kindle Fire 10 can offer you a decent sound in all apps that you normally use. It can make listening to music or videos and conducting conversations easy enough. The volume can be adjusted by tapping the gear on the top right of your screen and adjusting using the slider.

Sliding to the right turns it up and sliding it left turns it down.

One thing I noticed about this tablet is that sound on Skype is oddly lower than all other apps. This makes it hard to participate in normal conversations. You may want to consider using some amplifying headphones if you use Skype often. A software fix will help this issue hopefully soon.

While I never had this problem, many people online have reported issues with sound going out. There is an amplitude of sound fixes on the tablet. You can also use a product protection plan or a factory reset to restore sound. This issue may or may not affect you. It is not the sort of fix that you should let deter you from considering this tablet, but you should be aware that they may affect you later on. This seems to be something quite unique to Android devices.

There is also a speaker boost app available on the Amazon App Store, designed specifically for devices like this one. So if you like your beats plat and your bass down low, you can try this app! The app warns, "Use at your own risk." Listening to loud music for too long of a period can be detrimental to your hearing. But you probably already knew that. So use at your own risk and enjoy even greater sound.

Storage

Storage is important because it's what you save everything on. It stores your pictures, your apps, your videos, and anything else you want to save. It can also save apps that you don't have room for on the device itself. The Kindle Fire 10 has options of 32 GB or 64 GB. You can store up to 8192 photos on 32 GB (Voo, 2018). Or you can store up to double that on 64. Consider your needs when you select which storage capacity you want. Do you just browse the web, use Facebook, and send emails to friends? The lower size is for you. Do you take pictures and edit them on this device? In that case, go with the largest size and consider backup storage too.

On top of this, you can insert your own MicroSD card. Be sure to buy the micro size; others won't fit on this device. The largest size you can buy is 128 GB. Having an SD card this big can really help you store larger files, like video files, but a 32 or 64 GB card is sufficient for things like photos, word files, and other smaller files that the average user needs.

RAM and Processor

To handle all of your needs, the Kindle Fire 10 has made some significant upgrades to its processor. While you may not understand what exactly has happened, until of course you realize that it is faster and smoother when switching between apps.

In simple English, a processor just computes everything. It basically runs your tablet. A more efficient processor will be able to compute more quickly and smoothly. So your functions, from loading apps to switching between them, is affected. Now your RAM is your internal memory, or Random Access Memory. It stores information that the processor accesses to perform its calculations. CPU, or your processor, is more important in the long run because a faster and better CPU can help you access more RAM and utilize it. Your RAM may be all that, but it's useless without a great processor. Having lots of RAM is beneficial only if you have a processor that can utilize all of it as needed.

The Kindle Fire 10 has a MediaTek quad-core chip paired with 2GB of RAM. According to Amazon, this is thirty percent faster than the original chip in older Kindle Fire versions. This means that using this tablet will be thirty percent faster. Of course you can't quantify the speed you notice, but you will see the difference in how fast you can close out a window and bring up another app, or how fast you can load a WebPage, or how fast you can download and upload files. If someone emails you something, you will notice that you can open the file more quickly. You can close an app and bring up another one with less effort and lag. So for you, your work and your entertainment become speedier and easier. And that is just what you would expect from a tablet.

If you have owned a previous Kindle Fire, you may have noticed that it is not as great as this one. You can't expect as much power, speed, or efficiency. The Kindle Fire 10 offers a much better processor which offers much better performance.

Apps

What's a tablet without decent apps? You want to have access to all the functions you want to use this device for. So what can your Kindle Fire 10 do for you?

This tablet runs on the Fire OS, the custom version of Android created by Amazon. While this is not bad software, it can have its issues. This we cover in more depth in following chapters. This interface allows you to switch between the launcher and apps and interact with the device. Generally, the interface is very straightforward, easy to use, and effortless.

There is an interesting "For You" part which helps you find the apps you recently used and suggests more apps for you. This section can be especially useful for someone who forgets things easily, or who can't navigate and explore the tablet easily on his or her own.

Chapter 1: What It's Like

There are apps built into the device just for videos, books, music, games, magazines, and audiobooks. All of your downloaded content will appear in these sections. You will also find that the Kindle Fire 10 comes with its own suite of apps, such as a calendar, email, contacts, and documents. You can utilize these for work. Using the apps that come with the device offer the best performance, but you may find that they are limited in their capabilities. Downloading other apps, or accessing them through the web browser built into the device, may be a better option for you. For instance, if you are used to using Gmail, you may not enjoy switching to the built-in email, so you should consider accessing Gmail through the web browser by going to Google.

You can also use Alexa on your Kindle Fire 10! Just hold the home button down until a blue line appears. This means that Alexa is ready and waiting for your commands. Teach your voice and she will respond to it exclusively. In case you didn't know, Alexa is a voice-controlled app that will perform tasks for you based on your voice. You can turn Alexa on by talking to her and saying, "Hey, Alexa." Alexa is one of the newest options in digital assistance, offered by Amazon to compete with such other devices such as Google's or Apple's Siri. Talk to her and she will recognize your voice and obey your commands. Alexa is already built into your Kindle, you just have to activate it.

To open a new app, just hit the home button and then locate the app icon of the app you want to open. Tap on it and it will open.

Chapter 1: What It's Like

To go through apps that are currently running on the device, just hit the Home button twice. This will activate Quick Switch. Swipe up on items that you don't want to use, and tap on recently opened items to open them. Swiping up helps you close items that you don't want to use right now. It helps you preserve battery life that way because it ensures that the apps aren't just running in the background without being used. But don't worry, swiping up won't delete or remove the app from your device. You can always access it later when you do need it.

Unfortunately, you can only access apps through the Amazon App Store, which does not offer as much as Google Play Store or Apple's App Store. This app store is sufficient for your basic needs…Netflix, Hulu, email plugins, and the like. You should find what you need here. It simply doesn't offer the popular Google apps you may need, such as Gmail or Youtube.

To download apps, just open the app store on your device, tap on the search bar, and enter the name of the app you want. When you find the app you are seeking, tap on it and press "Download." You can also browse the apps listed on the store to find ones you may want. The device will start to download it and then install it. The app icon will automatically appear on your home page, where you can access it later.

The Kindle Fire 10 can hold many apps, depending on the storage you select. Remember that each app you download will take up storage space. If you use and switch between a lot of apps, you need to go for the 64 Gb size Kindle or install a MicroSD card. You will eat through storage pretty fast the more apps you download.

Switching between apps is easy and effortless. You won't notice lag or freezing. This is because the processor can easily handle a decent workload. It can switch between apps as needed.

Camera

Yes, the Kindle Fire 10 has a camera! So if you are using your device and you see an amazing sunset or a sweet bird, you can snap a picture of it. If you are looking especially cute today, you can also snap a nice selfie. How convenient is that? Plus, both cameras are useful for video chats and Skype calls, where you can show someone your face or the scene around you.

This camera is nothing fancy. You probably won't be winning National Geographic photo contests with your nature photos taken on this device. But it can document your world and let you save pictures that mean a lot to you.

With two megapixels, it's basically as good as any phone camera. Expect the same quality. Unless your lighting is excellent, pictures will be grainy. The tablet is also not able to account for shaking or instability, so be sure to have it steady before you snap a picture.

There is also flash to add brightness to the scene you want to shoot. Using flash can

Chapter 1: What It's Like

alter images, such as creating red eyes. You want to be careful using it for this reason. You can set autoflash, where the camera will use it when it determines it needs it, or you can set no flash or flash.

To access the camera, simply tap on the favorites grid and you will see the camera app icon, tap on that. Your screen will fill with the scene in front of you. When you find the picture you want to take, tap the little camera aperture button on the bottom of the camera app. It will snap the picture.

You can also switch to the front-facing camera. This shows what is in front of the screen, instead of behind it. You will see a little icon on the bottom left of your camera screen when you open the app. Tap on that to switch which camera you use. Taking a shot this way is the same as taking a shot with the rear-facing camera.

When you want to view the pictures you have taken, you can simply access them by tapping on the little thumbnail of the image at the bottom right of your screen. Go through your pictures to edit them or delete them. You can also change where you wish to save them this way. You will find that the editing tools on the Kindle Fire 10 are somewhat limited to cropping, changing the lighting, or altering the orientation.

Battery

Clearly battery life is important because you want to be able to use your device without the charger and on the go. Being tied down to a charger all of the time means that you might as well just be using a desktop computer. Fortunately, the battery in this device should last you a good ten hours while using the device for various things.

Obviously, some things will kill battery life faster than others. Let's look at what may drain your battery faster.

Taking pictures will often require more battery than anything else. This is because your camera will make the device work harder and thus pull more power from the battery.

Using apps with lots of plugins, images, and other media can eat into your battery life. These apps include social media, such as Facebook or Instagram.

Games have a lot of display requirements, and can alter the brightness of your device. This makes your Kindle work harder, which eats into the battery life. You will notice that your battery will go down more when you play lots of games.

Your display will require a lot of battery. Turning the brightness down can really help you save battery. If you know that you are about to go on a long car ride or flight and you won't be able to plug in, you should turn the brightness of your display down. Turning the brightness down is as easy as opening your settings and using a slider to adjust the brightness up or down. Remember, more brightness means less battery.

Chapter 1: What It's Like

Playing videos can also drain the battery. You will notice a bite is taken out of the battery percentage when you watch various videos, or movies on Netflix, or TV episodes on Hulu.

Leaving apps running in the background can kill your battery without you knowing why. If your battery appears to drain rather quickly, just close all the apps you aren't using. A good habit is to close an app when you don't need it any longer. Closing an app won't delete it from your device so don't worry.

To save battery life, you want to have a darker background. Lighter backgrounds will take up more power to keep lit. You also want to turn down the brightness. You can always adjust it back up if you need a brighter screen for a moment. Close apps when you are done with them (there is a guide as to how to do this under the above section called "Apps"). Finally, avoid using things like movie apps or watching videos or playing games when you know you need to save your battery for a long time.

Appearance

You may wonder what this tablet looks like. Well, it is a rectangular and sleek device. It has a hard matte plastic finish on the back and a sleek glass screen on front. It is available in blue, black, or red.

It only weighs about fifteen ounces. This feels like holding a slim book or a heavy magazine. It is lightweight enough to make it incredibly convenient.

Chapter 1: What It's Like

Now if you don't like this standard Kindle, you can customize it. There is a great Folio case available on Amazon for only $39.99. You can also find cheaper used ones on places like eBay. Check out customizable skins with cool patterns as well. Make this device uniquely yours. Even if you don't like how it looks, you can still make it what you want.

You can also customize your background and set pictures that you like in place of the standard pictures offered on the device.

It's pretty hard to hold this device in just one hand. You will probably need two. Investing in a kickstand to prop it up to watch videos or partake in video chats can also be helpful.

Budget

Well, if nothing else matters, you should know that owning this tablet is a break on your wallet! For only one hundred and fifty bucks, this tablet can be yours. That is a significant value, considering what this tablet offers versus what others offer for a much higher price. Compared to $300 for a new iPad, you could be saving a lot of money and still getting a great and functional tablet with advanced capabilities.

Chapter 2: Setting Up Your Tablet

So you just got your Kindle Fire 10. That's great, but now what? Well, now you want to set up this device to do what you want. Setting up your Kindle Fire 10 is fairly easy but here you will find explicit instructions on how to do it. You can make this device work how you want it to and customize it to make it easier for your own use. Put apps where you can easily find them, make the device look the way you want, activate Alexa, and download apps you need. Create calendar events and activate your email. All of this and more can be done on your new device! Read on to find out how.

Choosing Settings

First, charge your device. When it has a full charge, unplug it and turn it on. Now you will be prompted to enter settings, such as the language you wish to use. You can go through these settings quite easily on your own, as they are self-explanatory.

But now you are on your home screen. There are other aspects of set-up that you may need to follow now. You may want to set up a new picture, for instance, or you may want to change the language. All of this can be accomplished under "Settings." Swipe the notifications bar down and then use that to find the different settings. You can change the volume, brightness, notification sounds, display, language, accessibility, and every other part of your user experience under settings. To change your picture, you need to first take a picture or download one from the Internet.

Registering Your Device

To use your Kindle, you need to register it first with your Amazon account. On your home screen, swipe the notifications bar down and tap on "More." Then find "My Account." There, enter your Amazon account information. If you don't have an Amazon account, you can always sign up for one. But you need one to use this device.

Alexa

Alexa, Amazon's own digital assistant, is already installed in your device. You just have to activate her. To do this, hold down the home button until a blue line appears. Then you can give a command or ask her a question. It's as easy as pie.

Adding Email and Other Accounts

To fully personalize your Kindle Fire 10, you obviously want to hook up your personal accounts. You can do this by going to Settings. Then find "My Account." There will be a button for "Manage Email Accounts." Tap on this and you will find a way to enter your account and username and password. You can also create a new email account to associate with this device if you don't wish to sync up your email.

You can add social media to your Kindle Fire 10. For things like Facebook, you will have to download the app from the Amazon App Store. Connect to WiFi so that you can do this. Download the apps you want from the store.

Then tap on the app icons on your home screen and you will find a prompt for your email and password. Enter that, and you're in!

Creating Calendar Events

Your calendar keeps you organized, so you may want to set it up on your new device. To create a new calendar event, first open your calendar. Then scroll until you see the day you want to set up the event for. Tap on that day. A New Event Form will then appear. Fill out the information and select the time and date by tapping on those buttons. You can use the "repeat" button to make this event repeat if it is recurring. You will have options for how often it repeats, including a customized option that allows you to set a unique repeating time as well as an end time if the event is not indefinitely repeating. You can also set reminders and customize those as well. Finally, tap save and the event will appear in your calendar.

Downloading Apps

I already spoke about downloading apps. Well, how do you do that?

First, you need to open the App Store, which should be an icon on your home screen. Then look up the app you want, tap on "Download." When it downloads, it will automatically install. You can then tap "Open" to access the app. Or you can close the store and access the app through the icon that appears on your home screens.

Now, the Amazon App Store is notoriously limited. So you can combat this by

Chapter 2: Setting Up Your Tablet

downloading Google and other Android apps onto your device. You just have to open settings, then find security, then toggle the button that says "Apps from Unknown Sources" to on. Then you can look up apps on the Google Play Store on your web browser and download them onto your tablet. Just be careful to only download Play Store apps, because otherwise you may get an app from an untrustworthy source. Alternatively, download Google Play Store from the web and access new apps through that app.

Hooking up to WiFi

To hook your tablet up to WiFi, you have to first open "Quick Settings" from the dropdown menu from the top. Then find "Wireless." Make sure that you don't accidentally have Airplane Mode on, as that mode will block all signals from reaching your device. Then tap the button next to WiFi so that it is on. Find a network you want to connect to and tap on it. When you see the lock icon that means you need to enter a password; your device will prompt you if you need to do this. Enter the password and then hit "Connect." After you connect once, your Kindle should connect every time it comes into range of this network.

Getting Games and Other Content

You can retrieve most content you need through your Amazon account. There will be sections on your device for things like video, music, and eBooks. You can also go onto your Amazon account and purchase this content and have it sent to your device. Since your device is registered with your Amazon account, your content will automatically be accessible on the device provided it has WiFi connection. Otherwise, you may need to move content from your computer to your tablet via USB cable.

Chapter 3: Display Issues

Now when you get a new device, you want to enjoy it without any hassle. But as with all electronics, things do go wrong. Being able to take care of any issues that may spring up will help you continue enjoying this device without any more headache, it can also save you the money of expensive repairs or getting a new device. Most issues are fixable, but you simply have to learn how to fix them yourself. There is seldom any need to use your warranty or return your device or hire an expensive professional to fix simple issues that you may encounter.

One of the most common issues that you may face involves the screen and the display. Many users have dealt with these issues, as have I. A black screen, a glitchy display, cracks – they happen from time to time. Learning how to fix these issues can help you restore the display you count on to use this device properly and enjoy your content.

Let's cover some of these potential issues and what to do about them.

Screen Stays Black

If the screen stays black, reboot the device by holding the power button down for at least twenty seconds. Then turn it back on. Also make sure you have a full charge. If these things don't work, something is seriously

Chapter 3: Display Issues

wrong and you need to contact Amazon for a replacement.

Screen Flickers

If you notice that the screen flickers, you should check a few things. This is likely caused by the brightness setting.

Change the Brightness

Pull down the notifications bar and then adjust brightness. Also turn Auto Brightness to off. You want to be able to customize brightness yourself.

Remove the Cover

Take off your cover. It may be interfering with the brightness setting and toggling it without you realizing it.

Get a Replacement

If the above tips don't help, it may be time to seek a replacement. Sorry!

Screen Haze

One issue that some people report with the Kindle Fire 10 is a blue or purple haze around the edges of their device screens when the background is white. This haze is more annoying than anything, but fixing it is preferable.

If there is a minor haze that you can ignore, consider it just part of owning this tablet. The blue LEDs that are part of this device cause the haze. You may find that using the tablet in well-lit areas can help diminish this problematic effect.

However, if the haze limits your visibility or destroys images, then you need to contact Amazon for a free replacement. It is a manufacturer's flaw which you can get replaced for no extra charge.

Chapter 4: Battery Issues

Your battery is the powerhouse of the whole device. Without the battery working, you might as well not even own a tablet! The Kindle Fire 10 is prone to a few battery issues that you must fix in order to keep using your tablet. Usually these battery issues are related to software or charger issues, and not the device itself.

Refusing to Charge

Generally, charging issues have to do with the charger and not the tablet itself. When your device refuses to charge or charges very slowly, you must remember some basic facts about using your device. For one thing, you should be using a charger that is compatible with the device. The best charger is the special Kindle charger, available through Amazon for $20. This charger will charge your device in four hours. You can also use your USB cable connected to your computer, but that generally will take up to fourteen hours to charge. All other chargers will probably be slower.

Reboot, Then Charge

Hold the power button down for twenty seconds. When the device is fully off, you can then connect the charger. Sometimes doing this helps kill all programs so that the device is more receptive to charging.

Chapter 4: Battery Issues

Check Your Charger

The rating of your charger will influence how fast your device charges up. You may have a charger with a low rating which will naturally be slower in charging. It is best to use the charger that came with your device or buy the Amazon Kindle PowerFast for Accelerated Charging to get lightening fast charging.

Try a New Charger

The USB cables that come with chargers often will wear out over time. They may lose their ability to charge altogether. Outlets in the house may also give out, or the charging box will lose the ability to keep up a smooth and speedy charge. So if you want to charge your device and it's not charging, then you may try changing chargers, outlets, or power sources. The problem is more likely to lie in the charger than in the device. Also try switching from wall outlets to using your computer. If charging on your computer, the problem may lie in the USB port you are plugged into, so be sure to try different USB ports.

Check the Charging Port

The charging port is where the charger connects to the device. This little hole has prongs inside of it that conduct the electricity from the charger. Sometimes, these prongs can become bent, which inhibits the charging process. Hold your device up and peek into the charging port to see if the prongs are somehow messed up or something is blocking them, such as gunk or debris.

Chapter 4: Battery Issues

To fix this, you can take a bobby pin and reach into the hole to straighten the prongs out or clean out any debris. You must be very delicate about this, or you may break the prongs and thus void your warranty. The prongs are quite fragile.

Get a Replacement

A replacement is in order when your device refuses to charge no matter what. The issue here is likely within the tablet itself, such as a broken charging port or a damaged battery that cannot take a charge. You must have this issue fixed or the whole device replaced if other measures don't take care of the problem.

Also be very careful never to get your tablet wet. Getting it wet can damage the internal hardware, leading to charging problems. There is more advice on what to do if you get it wet later in this chapter. A replacement is likely in order if you completely submerge the device.

Overheating

Sometimes, the Kindle Fire 10 will overheat while playing games and other content that requires a lot of CPU and battery power. When this happens, you risk destroying the battery. It is imperative that you stop whatever you are doing, shut the tablet off, and let it cool off. Stopping the overheating issues before they effectively destroy your device and the hardware inside is further imperative.

Chapter 4: Battery Issues

Naturally, the tablet will produce heat as it works. The cooling fan and other technology within the device will get rid of this heat, keeping the temperature at a safe level for the battery. When the technology cannot keep up with the heat being generated, it will overheat and create unsafe conditions for the battery. Then the device will stop working and may even shut down to protect itself.

You can tell the device is overheating because it will feel hot for one thing. But you will also notice that it is struggling to compute as normal, and it is churning, trying hard to work. It may freeze up. It may also send you a warning about the dangerous temperature level or shut down to protect itself. When the tablet is too hot to touch comfortably, you know that there is a problem.

Check Your Software

More often than not, overheating is caused by a software program on the tablet that is forcing the tablet to work way too hard. Often, this program will freeze and make the CPU work in a loop. The CPU is struggling so hard to keep up that it glitches and the tablet struggles to compensate by working harder than it should. So, when your tablet overheats, first consider checking the software. Have you installed any new apps lately that seemed to start the problem? Did the problem start after you put some file or app on the device? Does it only overheat when you are using certain programs or playing certain games?

The easy solution here is to find the program causing the issue and then deleting it

Chapter 4: Battery Issues

from the device. You can install it again later and see if it works better.

If you have no clue which app is causing the problem, you can try eliminating apps one by one. First delete ones that take up a lot of CPU space. You can see how much they take by viewing the app settings. See if the problem goes away. If it persists, try deleting the next app. Do this until you get rid of the problem.

Avoid Overcharging

When the battery reaches 100%, immediately take it off the charger. Sometimes letting the battery die is actually healthy for it. Overcharging can wear out the battery and may even lead to overheating, since charging generates heat on its own.

Seek a Replacement

If you have tried the above with no luck, then it may be time to contact Amazon for a replacement tablet. This should not be happening, so it suggests a manufacturing glitch is present. A new tablet is the only solution in this case. It will be provided free of charge if the issue lies in manufacturing and not damages you yourself did to the tablet.

Getting It Wet

It's not too uncommon to get your Kindle Fire 10 wet. For instance, you are walking along a pretty lake with your dog and watching cute dog videos on Youtube. Your German Shepherd sees a squirrel and yanks on the leash really hard. You tumble head first over your feet and your tablet flies out of your hands, right into the lake. You dive after it but the damage is already done.

The bad news is that getting your tablet wet can create massive electronic problems. It can even stop the screen and battery from functioning. The good news is, there is a quick fix you can try before getting rid of the tablet.

First, DO NOT, I repeat, DO NOT turn it on. Turing it on will let the damage set in. It can also cause the tablet to short out. If it is on, then turn it off.

Next, wipe it dry on the outside with a towel or cloth. Be sure to remove it from the case and dry it off that way. Make sure the whole thing is completely dry on the outside.

Now get a gallon-sized storage bag. Fill your bag with four to six cups of dry rice. The rice cannot be cooked because cooked rice has moisture. Put your tablet in this bag, squeeze out all of the excess air, and then ziplock it shut. Shake the bag to make sure that your tablet is totally covered in rice.

Let it sit overnight. Twenty-four hours is even better. Take it out, wipe off the rice dust that may have accumulated, and try powering it on. It should turn on! The rice sucks the moisture out of it and prevents further damage from being done. It's like magic!

This handy trick also works with other electronic devices, like phones. Since it is not unusual to accidentally get your electronics wet,

Chapter 4: Battery Issues

you can save this in your back pocket for when you need it. You probably will need it someday.

Chapter 5: Software and Connectivity Issues

The Kindle Fire 10's most common issues usually involve software or connectivity. These issues are unfortunately the most frustrating because they limit or even ruin your tablet experience. Fortunately, these issues are also typically the easiest to find and fix. Software issues are usually as simple as deleting a problematic app or rebooting the device. You may even need to factory reset if problems persist. You can usually doctor the device entirely yourself should there be software problems.

App Crashing

When an app crashed but your device works fine, that means there is something wrong with the app, not your Kindle. The best thing to do in this case is to address the app itself.

Clear Data

First, go to settings. Then open applications and tap on "Manage All Applications." Here, find the name of the malfunctioning app. Tap on "Clear Data." This will usually help the app resolve its own issues. You can also try "Clear Cache."

Remove Parental Controls

Chapter 5: Software and Connectivity Issues

Parental controls can block or crash the browser. So to clear them, go to Settings and then to Parental Controls. There, turn parental controls off.

Delete the App

If all else fails, you need to delete the app. You can do this by going to settings and then "Manage All Applications." Open the app that is giving you trouble and then tap "Uninstall." You can try installing it again later to see if it behaves now.

Freezing During Use

You are using your tablet like you always do. Suddenly, it stops responding. It is stuck on one page and nothing you do changes it. It won't respond to your taps. It starts to act funky, possibly freezing or switching between pages without any direction from you. This infuriating problem is typically caused by software glitching.

Reboot

Hold down on the power button for twenty seconds, until your screen goes black. It should then restart. See if it works better now. Sometimes, a reboot is all you need to close a troublesome program and get the device running again.

Eliminate Problem Software

Often, freezing is caused by a software not working right. You can address this issue by deleting apps that seem to cause the freezing

Chapter 5: Software and Connectivity Issues

issue. First, see if using any particular apps seems to make your device freeze a lot. Second, notice if the issue has started since you downloaded or deleted a certain app. Now delete that app and see if the problem improves. You can download the software again later to see if it works better.

Download Software You Deleted

Certain programs that are on your device when you get it help the device run properly. Deleting them is a mistake. Be sure to note all of the software you take off of or disable on your device. If your device stops working properly following the disabling of an app, you should enable or re-download the app. You may need to do this on the computer and port it to your device if the freezing issues are so bad that you can't even access the Amazon App Store.

Failure to Start Up

So you are eager to watch a movie and you go to turn your tablet on, and then nothing happens. It refuses to boot up. You can't get it to start even though the battery is fully charged. You naturally get frustrated – you paid money to have a working tablet and this one doesn't even want to turn on! What can you do in this scenario? Well, never fear; all hope is not lost.

Check Your Battery

Maybe you think it's charged since you have been charging it. But your charger may be faulty and the battery never got a charge at all.

Chapter 5: Software and Connectivity Issues

Try changing chargers and using a simple phone charger. Or try changing outlets, just in case your outlet is faulty. You should then leave it for an hour to see if there has been a change.

Reboot

Sometimes, the lack of booting is related to a software issue. A hard reboot can save you from this tablet user's nightmare. Simply hold down on the power button for twenty seconds. Your tablet should turn on at this point.

Not Connecting to PC

Many users have reported issues connecting their Kindle Fire 10's to the PC. This issue can be frustrating, especially when you need to move content from your PC to your tablet with a minimum of frustration. You may find that the tablet does not show up under your "computer" files, or that you get an error message when you try to move files.

To remove the frustration, try these tips.

Restart

Whenever you encounter a problem with your computer or tablet, the first step is to try restarting. Hold the power button your computer and your tablet for twenty seconds to reboot both devices. Then try again. It may just work this time.

Change USB Cable

Chapter 5: Software and Connectivity Issues

Perhaps the problem is your cable. Try using a different one. Sometimes, cables get damaged or old and stop communicating between devices properly.

Change Ports

The problem may also lie in the port you are attempting to use. You can unplug your tablet and insert in a different port. See if it works now.

Install the Right Driver

If your tablet just is not showing up on your computer, you may not have the correct driver to read your device on your PC. Without the right driver, your tablet won't show up on the computer at all. You can have the right cord and everything but it won't work without the right software on your computer. Look up free Kindle Fire 10 drivers and install them on your PC. Be sure to restart your PC before you hook up the tablet to try again. Now, after restarting the PC, try to see what happens when you plug in your tablet this time.

Also, always be sure to have the Media Transfer Protocol Porting Kit installed on your computer. Without this kit, you won't be able to transfer files between your computer and any other device. This porting kit is free and can be found online or in your Windows web store. It is useful for more than just your tablet so be sure you have it.

Use Dropbox Instead

Chapter 5: Software and Connectivity Issues

If you can't get your tablet to connect, consider that you can skip the PC-to-tablet altogether. You can do this by downloading Dropbox onto your PC for free. Then move all of the files that you want to transfer to your tablet onto your Dropbox. You can store up to two GB for free on Dropbox.

Once you have moved the files, open up Dropbox on your tablet. Sign in with the email and password you used to create your account on your PC. Then open up the files you want to transfer and tap "Download." This will download these files onto your tablet without any problems.

Note: You need to use WiFi to accomplish this.

Not Connecting to WiFi

You really need WiFi to connect to the Internet and get the content you need. A tablet is no fun without WiFi. So what should you do if you can't connect?

Reboot

The first thing to do is to shut off your Kindle and also your router. Then restart them both. See if that resolves the issue. Nine times out of ten, if your WiFi is wonky, you can repair it simply by restarting the router.

Check Your WiFi

Download a free WiFi Analyzer app from your Amazon App Store. This will analyze your WiFi and find out if there is anything wrong with it. Maybe you have a busy signal, or a poor connection. Test out your WiFi before you blame the tablet.

Reconnect

When you connect to WiFi, you sign into the network. Sometimes, your tablet may configure the settings improperly later on. You can fix this simply by disconnecting from the network and then connecting again. You may or may not have to go through the sign-in process again. It is best to tell your tablet to "forget" the network by tapping the "Forget" button. Going through the whole sign-in process can be a pain but it might restore your connectivity.

Factory Reset

It is never pleasant to factory reset a tablet and get rid of all of the content you have put on there. But provided that you have backed this content up somewhere else, such as Dropbox or your computer, then you may have to do this.

First, ensure your tablet is fully charged.

Second, pull down the notifications bar and tap More and then My Account and then Deregister. You will have to read some text and select "Deregister" again. Or you can reset it from your computer by going into Amazon and clicking on Manage Your Content and Devices. Then select "Your Devices." Select your tablet and go to Actions. Select Deregister. Then get on your tablet and pull down the notifications bar and hit more, then device, then reset to

Chapter 5: Software and Connectivity Issues

factory defaults and confirm by tapping "Erase everything." When you restart, you will have to enter the WiFi and sign into the network again. You will also have to download all content again.

Chapter 6: Sound Issues

The sound in your device is not just related to the speakers. It can also be related to your software. Certain software in the device controls the sound that gets to the speaker and makes the speakers work. If you have any sound issues, you likely have to address the software. But whether the software or the speakers are at fault, you can fix this issue yourself.

No Sound

No sound through the headphones or speakers is one of the most common issues that users report with their tablets. I have even had this issue. You go to talk to your friend from Hong Kong and...nada! She is moving her mouth but you can't hear a word. It's infuriating to say the least. So what can you do about it?

Make Sure Your Volume Is Up

This seems so obvious that you may wonder why I'm mentioning it. But you may have muted the device without realizing it. Check the volume slider and slide it up.

It May Be the Headphones

If you remove the headphones while your tablet is asleep, it may believe the headphones are still in. So try plugging your

Chapter 6: Sound Issues

headphones in again and then removing them. This may jolt the device into realizing that they aren't there anymore.

Clean the Headphone Jack

Maybe some gunk got into the headphone jack, which is messing with your headphones. Try cleaning it out with a Q-tip. Don't wet the Q-tip.

The Case Is in the Way

The case may be preventing the headphones from getting a good connection. Try removing the case and inserting the headphones again.

Reboot

As always, a hard reboot can help. Try rebooting the device by holding the power button down until it shuts off. Then turn it back on. The problem may sort itself out this way if it is a software defect.

Get a Replacement

Your speakers or headphone jack may be faulty. You can tell that this is the problem if you hear static or distortion. You may also notice it if you have to jiggle the headphones just to get sound. To fix this issue, you will have to contact Amazon.

Chapter 7: Hardware Issues

In this chapter, we will cover hardware issues not related to your battery or speakers. Hardware refers to parts of your device that are hard – essentially, the machine parts that make the tablet what it is. The different parts work together to keep the device functioning properly. Any issues with any of these parts can lead to issues with the device overall. It cannot function without its proper hardware components, no matter how great the software is. Therefore, you want to ensure that the device continues to run properly by fixing any hardware issues that you may encounter.

MicroSD Card Not Working

You insert a MicroSD card and now it won't work. The device won't recognize it for some reason.

Turn It Off and Remove It

Turn the device off completely. Then take out the card. Put the card back in and boot the device back up. See if this helps.

Update Drivers

An outdated software can cause this problem. Make sure your tablet is fully charged and shut it down. Then boot it up while connected to WiFi. It should force itself to download necessary updates that can read your card.

Reformat the Card

Remove the card from your tablet and put it into your computer. Go to computer files and find the card. Right click on it and reformat it. Keep in mind that reformatting will erase all data on the disk, so you want to make sure anything you want to keep is safely backed up.

Shutting Down on Its Own

Does your tablet seem to have a mind of its own? A lot of people have reported their tablets shutting off on their own. If you have this problem, there are a few things you can try.

Screen Timeout

This could be a settings problem. So go to "Settings" and then find Display, tap on

"Screen Timeout." Then set it to Never or something that agrees with you. Otherwise, the screen will shut off by itself.

Factory Reset

If your tablet is charged and the issue is not your display settings, then you need to back up the device. Then reset it by making sure it is charged. Then pull down the notifications bar and tap More and then My Account and then Deregister. You will have to read some text and select "Deregister" again. Or you can reset it from your computer by going into Amazon and clicking on Manage Your Content and Devices. Then select "Your Devices." Select your tablet and go to Actions. Select Deregister. Then get on your tablet and pull down the notifications bar and hit more, then device, then reset to factory defaults and confirm by tapping "Erase everything."

Keyboard Typing Erratically

This is another issue many users have reported. You can fix it in a few different ways, depending on the cause of the issue.

Clean the Keyboard Well

Wipe it down with a microfiber cloth. This will clear any debris that may be causing the keys to stick down and type on their own.

Reboot

You may have to reboot. And if that doesn't work, escalate by factory resetting it.

And if that still doesn't help, well, it's time to contact Amazon for a replacement.

Chapter 8: Caring for Your Device

A lot of problems that you may have with your Kindle Fire 10 can be prevented by simply caring for your device properly. Before you run into trouble with your Kindle Fire 10, why not take care of it? That way, you can save a lot of heartache and hassle. A few bucks on preventative maintenance is often a lot cheaper than having to buy a new tablet or fork out money for repairs. Read on to find out how to care for your device properly so that it lasts for years to come. Or at least until the next model is out!

Invest in a Case

To preserve the exterior of your device, a case is the best option. Investing in a case can really make a difference in how you care for your tablet and it can protect your tablet. Think about it. Just normal use will create scratches and wear and tear that damage the cosmetic appearance. And if you drop your device, you may crack the exterior or – gulp! – the screen. A case prevents all of that by creating a shell that protected and preserves the device underneath.

Plus, cases look cool and can let you customize the outward appearance of your device. You can express your own personality that way. There's another plus to buying one.

Chapter 8: Caring for Your Device

Before purchasing a case, make sure that it is actually made for the Kindle Fire 10. Older Kindle cases won't fit right. You want to make sure it is specifically for this version. That is the only way you can ensure you get a case that fits right and offers the best protection, while also leaving holes for the camera, headphones, charger, and other jacks. Any other case may block these things and minimize the convenience of using your tablet.

Amazon is the best place to find cases, since they are the manufacturer of this device. But you can find cases on eBay and other stores as well. Leather and rubber are probably the best materials, as they offer the most protection from dropping. Remember that cheaper is not always better. You want to spend more and get good protection than spend less and gets something that falls apart within two weeks. Reading reviews is a good way to ensure the quality of what you are buying.

Invest in Screen Protection

A broken screen is always an icky issue to deal with in electronics. Not only can it obliterate your viewing experiences, but it lowers the value of your Kindle and makes typing and swiping a potentially bloody nightmare. Your Kindle Fire 10 is no exception when it comes to the fragile glass screen. To protect your screen, you need to invest in some quality screen protection. This screen protection will ensure that nothing can crack your screen. That improves your overall tablet experience.

Chapter 8: Caring for Your Device

Most screen protectors are tempered glass screens that you fit over your original screen. They come sized specifically for the tablet. Amazon carries a few products for this.

Installing the screen protection is not too difficult. The hardest part is avoiding bubbles from forming under the glass when you lay it down. Make sure to use the little tool that comes with these screen protectors and press down to even it out and get rid of bubbles. Furthermore, you should line it up before putting it on to make sure that you get it even and don't have any overhang. It's not like you can trim glass to fit your size needs, so be sure to lay it down properly the first time.

Once the screen protector is on, realize that your screen is still not invincible. A fall from the Empire State Building will still obliterate the screen. You still want to exercise caution in handling the screen. But now you have an extra layer of protection. With most drops and falls, the screen protector will bear the brunt of the damage. The screen underneath will usually remain intact.

When you break the screen protector, it is best to replace it with a new one. Otherwise, its protective qualities will be compromised.

How to Clean

The more you use your device, the dirtier it will get. Dirt can even cause damage as it makes your screen hard to see through and clogs your headphone jacks and charging port. Keeping your device clean is important for preventative maintenance.

Chapter 8: Caring for Your Device

To clean your device, you should invest in some cleansing wipes. These are sold on Amazon. They are designed especially for cleaning electronics without leaving behind an annoying residue or damaging the hardware in any way. They are also convenient and work like a charm. Some people have reported that using baby wipes works just as well, but I have never chanced it. I always stick to actual electronic cleansing wipes. You can find a pack of 25 made by Windex on Amazon for just $25.

NEVER use water or cleaning chemicals to clean your device. Chemicals will destroy the device. Water can get inside of it and lead to electronic failure. Using these things will void your warranty and make it impossible to replace your device for no charge if anything happens to it as a result. You want to stick to special wipes made for electronic devices.

Watch Your Downloads

You know all about computer viruses. Well, your tablet is not immune to them, either. You can still get viruses that can steal your personal information, wipe out your memory, and make your device unusable. Removing viruses usually requires the help of a professional.

Avoiding viruses is usually pretty easy. Just follow these steps:

Know where you are downloading something from. Only download apps on the Amazon App Store, or you can void your

Chapter 8: Caring for Your Device

warranty. If you want to download a game or movie, be sure that it is from a reputable site.

Don't follow random links that people send you, or that pop up on your screen.

Avoid sites with lots of pop-up ads. These sites usually have poor security.

Avoid sites that you don't know. Unless they are reputable sites from companies you are familiar with, you want to avoid going to them.

Don't just download anything. It has to be a software, app, movie, song, or picture that you find on a reputable site.

Make sure your WiFi is a secure connection. People have been known to get hacked over their internet connections. Require a password and encryption.

Use virus protection. It is not 100% effective, but it is way better than having nothing at all. You can find virus protection, such as Lookout Mobile Security, in your app store. Lookout is helpful because you can also activate theft protection where it will scream if it has been stolen and you can locate your device on the computer if you lose it.

Don't give your social security number or credit card information freely online. Only do this over secure connections on websites you trust. If you can have the website avoid saving your info, please do so.

Chapter 8: Caring for Your Device

Be sure to not save your passwords. Leaving your password in the blank on sites leaves you vulnerable to people hacking into your personal information should your device ever be stolen.

If a download starts that you didn't authorize, immediately do a hard reboot to stop the download. Downloads should never start without your permission. If they do, you are likely getting a virus.

Use Security

Beyond virus protection, you also want to protect your security and your device from theft. Lookout is the best for this. But you also want to set a password to up the security on your device.

When you first get your device, be sure to set a password so that no one else can access the device. Be sure to come up with something that is not easy for others to guess. You want to stay away from easy passwords, like 123 or a band name. Instead, come up with an acronym that has meaning to you and is easy for you to remember. Now add some numbers, such as your birthday, to the end of the acronym. Also be sure to capitalize a random letter. Replacing letters with numbers is another good trick. For example, your password may have an L in it, so replace that L with a 1 that looks somewhat like it. You can also throw in some random symbols, such as exclamation points.

The next thing you need to do is download and install Lookout from your App

Chapter 8: Caring for Your Device

Store. Create an account that you can access from your home computer or laptop or even phone. That way, if your device is lost or stolen, you can locate it. You can also shut it down so that your personal information is kept private. Finally, you can make the device scream, which can deter thieves.

Of course, use common sense about your device. It is valuable so thieves may want it. Don't leave it hanging out of your bookbag and don't leave it unattended in an area with high traffic. It is best to hold onto it at all times, or else leave it locked up where others can't get to it.

How to Charge Your Device Properly

You may think that charging is as simple as plugging in your device and waiting. You may leave it plugged in overnight as you sleep, or plug it in for a few hours whenever it gets low. But these careless charging practices can actually hurt your tablet's battery and lead to future battery issues. Believe it or not, there is actually a safe way to charge your device that preserves the battery for a long time.

First, don't run your battery down and then charge it up. Have regular charging times, such as at night while you are asleep. Prevent the battery from ever getting empty and dying.

Instead of letting it run down and then charging up, charge it whenever it is getting low. Don't let the battery die. Charging in small spurts is better than letting it die and charging it all the way up.

Chapter 8: Caring for Your Device

Don't leave it on the charger longer than you have to. You can use a smart charging app or unplug it when the battery reaches 100%. Charging too long is not the worst thing you can do, but it can generate heat which can destroy the battery over time.

Don't let it charge in a hot room or hot car. It needs to be cool as it charges. Heat is the number one killer of batteries. That said, don't leave it under heat under any circumstances.

It is best to leave your device off as it charges. This helps prevent heat buildup, which can destroy your battery. It also helps your device charge faster. If you must use it while charging, though, you won't kill the battery.

Conclusion

This has been your guide to everything Kindle Fire 10! Now if you are a new user, you have the information you need to navigate this device with ease. Or if you are someone looking to purchase this, you will find all of the information and details necessary for making a sound purchase decision you can feel good about. Sleep with ease knowing that you will love this device and be able to fix even the tiniest issues with it.

The Kindle Fire 10 is the newest Kindle Fire. It has many improvements that make it superior to previous versions. Nevertheless, it does have some issues that you need to be aware of and be able to fix. This device is excellent for simple and basic tablet needs. For its low price of $150, you can get the emailing, picture viewing, video viewing, and even gaming that you need.

It has a decent display and a nice sound. It also has an improved processor and larger RAM that make it thirty percent faster than previous versions. You also learned about the various apps you can use, and how to run them. You learned about the battery and how to preserve its life.

Beyond that, you can also fix various issues. You can fix the no sound issues, which plague many users. You can also find out how to fix battery issues, display issues, and other such problems that you may run into. You will be able to fix most things that go wrong with this device. Just because something may go wrong does not mean that you need to give up and get rid of this device. You just need to learn how to fix it. Most fixes are very simple ones that you can perform yourself.

Finally, you can learn how to take care of this device to preserve its life. You don't want to shell out money only to lose this device within a short period of time. Learning how to tend to it properly can help you lengthen its life span.

Now you are all set! You can enjoy your new tablet without any hassle. Have fun!

Please leave a review on Amazon! Let others know what you think about this guide.

Thank you!

Printed in the USA
CPSIA information can be obtained
at www.ICGtesting.com
LVHW021411220923
758925LV00004B/434

9 781717 068071